A
Philadelphia
Catholic
in
King James's
Court

Discussion / Study Guide

Discussion/Study Guide
for
A Philadelphia Catholic in King James's Court

by Martin de Porres Kennedy

Published by
Lilyfield Press
W5180 Jefferson St.
Necedah, WI   54646
1-800-932-3051

Cover illustration by Mark Covell

Printed in the United States of America

ISBN: 0-9671492-2-3

Directions for Use

This guide contains a series of questions for each chapter of
A Philadelphia Catholic in King James's Court. These questions are
designed to be adaptable to a wide range of uses: written essay
questions, formal discussion questions, or as springboards to more
in-depth analyses.

Each question references the page number in the book where the
topic can be located. A brief answer to the question is also provided.
In some cases, this is a factual answer, which often includes citations
from Scripture and/or the Catechism of the Catholic Church (CCC)
to support it. Keep in mind, however, that these answers are by no
means all encompassing. Entire books have been written on many of
the topics, and students wishing to expand their knowledge in any
given area could do much additional research.

In other cases, the answers represent opinions offered from the
author's perspective. These are not meant to be definitive, but rather
are intended for stimulating open discussion or guiding teachers in
evaluating student responses.

The author welcomes specific comments about the content or format
of the study guide that may be of help in future editions. Suggestions
may be addressed to: familytrad@aol.com, or Lilyfield Press,
W5180 Jefferson St., Necedah, WI 54646.

Chapter 1

1. Have you ever been in a situation in which you had an opportunity to defend the Faith? What were the questions, comments, accusations, etc. that you faced? Did you feel confident in this situation?

   This question is meant as a good starting point for discussions about the topics addressed in the book. The more we can learn about our Faith, the more confident we will feel in defending it!

2. At Mick O'Shea's funeral, what does Uncle Les consider to be blasphemous, and why? (p.12)

   Many non-Catholics believe that Holy Communion is merely a symbolic representation of the Last Supper. They believe that it is irreverent of Catholics to claim that the bread and wine are actually the Body and Blood of Jesus. Some also believe that by offering the Body and Blood of Jesus in the Sacrifice of the Mass, that we are putting Christ repeatedly through the agony of the Crucifixion and implying that his "once for all" sacrifice on Calvary was insufficient.

   Of course, these accusations are untrue. See Chapter 12 for a more detailed discussion of the Eucharist.

3. What does Father McBride mean when he says that "a family shares the same flesh and blood"? (p.12) Is there more than one interpretation to this?

   We "share flesh and blood" in a physical sense when we are related genetically to others. We also "share flesh and blood" in a spiritual sense when we come together to partake of the precious Body and Blood of Christ in the Eucharist. We are brothers and sisters in Christ.

4. What does Uncle Les mean when he refers to the Catholic Church as the "religion of the Dark Ages"? (p.12)

   Many Protestants view the Church as being stuck in the Pre-Reformation era. They see the "colorful capes, the candles, the altar boys, the incense" as evidence of man-made traditions. Because they don't have an understanding of these traditions and how Scripture supports them, Protestants often view them as pagan innovations.

5. Why is calling a priest "Father" a problem for Uncle Les? What does he mean when he says this practice is in direct contradiction to Scripture? (p.12) Is it?

    Read Matthew 23:1-12 to see the passage used by Protestants to make this claim. Then study the verses cited below. When Jesus says, "Call no man father," and "Call no man teacher," the context shows his true meaning — that no one is to be so full of religious pride that he proposes his own teachings rather than those of our Lord. Also, the Bible shows many instances of Jesus and the Apostles referring to themselves and other spiritual leaders as "Father." (See Acts 7:2, 1 Cor 4:14-16, 1 Thes 2:11, 1 Tim 1:2, and Tit 1:4.) Note: this question is covered in more detail in the questions for Chapter 12.

6. How do Catholic funerals differ from non-Catholic ones? (p.15) Does the Catholic belief in Purgatory and the Communion of Saints make a difference in how we react to the death of a loved one?

    A Catholic funeral Mass does not include a eulogy because the focus is not on worldly accomplishments. The belief in Purgatory is soothing because we know that a loved one can be cleansed of imperfections and enter God's Kingdom perfectly. The funeral Mass allows us to pray for the soul of the deceased, thereby aiding him or her in that journey. The doctrine of the Communion of Saints holds that all members of Christ's body have the ability to assist each other spiritually, for nothing separates us from the love of Christ, not even death.

7. What about the sensual aspect of worship — the works of art, statues, incense, and holy water? Are these distractions or aids to worship? (p.12) Why are these sacramentals present in Catholic churches and homes? Are they biblical?

    The Bible has many examples of the use of material things being used for the greater glory of God and as means to aid our prayers. See the following verses:

6

Statues	Incense	Holy water
Ex 25:18-21	*Lk 1:10*	*Num 5:17*
Num 21:8-9	*Ps 141:2*	*Num 8:7*
1 Kings 6:23-35	*Ex 30:8*	
	Rev 5:8	
	Rev 8:3-4	

8. Contrast Uncle Les and Uncle Matty. Are both uncles concerned about their nephew? How does their concern for Michael differ? (p.7-9, 18-19)

   Uncle Matty is worried about Michael's education and eventual success in a profession — a worldly concern — while Uncle Les is more interested in Michael's spiritual well-being.

9. What do you think of Uncle Les's intention to provide spiritual leadership to Michael and his family? (p.18-19) Is it a good thing? Is Uncle Les justified or is he interfering?

   His intention is good. He sincerely desires to lead Michael and the whole family to the full truth of the Gospel. His error is his belief that the full truth of the Gospel can be found by any individual who studies the Bible earnestly. To believe we possess the truth and yet be unwilling or unenthusiastic about sharing it does not make sense. Primarily we should spread the Gospel through our example, but we do need to be ready to give answer as to why we believe the things we do.

Chapter 2

1. Tammy O'Shea is reading a book by Fulton Sheen, and Michael, the Chronicles of Narnia. (p.23) Does it matter what you choose to read, listen to, and look at?

   Yes! Consider your ultimate goal — to be with God in eternity. Books can edify us with stories of virtue, or be harmful to our souls when they glorify evil.

2. Is studying the Bible necessary to be a good Catholic? Give your thoughts on Uncle Matty's opinion that "That's what monks are for." (p.24)

   St. Jerome, who translated the Bible into the Latin Vulgate, said, "Ignorance of the Scriptures is ignorance of Christ." The Catechism further states that the Church "forcefully and specifically exhorts all the Christian faithful to learn the surpassing knowledge of Jesus Christ by frequent reading of the divine Scriptures" (CCC 133). While many virtuous people over the centuries did not have access to the Bible or were unable to read, we should be thankful that God's Word is so accessible to us today and should take advantage of that through Scripture reading, Bible study, commentaries, discussions, etc.

3. Michael would like to "save" people, but in a different way than his fire fighter father. (p.26) Jesus says that giving up one's life for another is the greatest love of all. Can people in any profession or way of life be involved in saving others?

   Yes. Remember we are members of the one Body of Christ. There is no such thing as a good thought, deed or action, which does not strengthen the Body. Likewise, sin hurts all members of the Body. (See CCC 953.)

4. Les got rid of his family's television set. (p.28) Is TV the temple of the devil? Can it be? How can Satan use TV to seduce his victims?

   A TV set, by itself, is neither good nor evil, but it does provide a medium whereby we expose our weaknesses to those who are more than willing to prey upon us for profit. To the extent that by our TV viewing we are indulging in scandal, the failings of others, sexual stimulation and titillation, gruesome fantasy and all the rest, we are packaging ourselves for delivery to Satan. Even athletic events, good movies, and news, if they distract us from our primary obligations, can be detrimental.

5. Is there a value in centering one's family life as much as possible in the home? (p.28)

From the standpoint of Catholic theology, the family is the basic social unit and the foundation of civilization. To the extent that Satan can undermine the family, he wreaks havoc on society. It seems he has made tremendous progress in the last couple of decades in our culture. Some families seem to spend little time at home. They often live highly compartmentalized lives — with each family member doing his or her own thing. Surely these families have less "glue" keeping them together than those who work, learn, and play together as much as possible (not to mention praying together!).

Chapter 3

1. Elijah tells Michael that he likes to keep chores to a minimum on Sunday. (p.35) What does the Church teach about "keeping the Lord's Day holy?"

   The Catechism says that "On Sundays and other holy days of obligation, the faithful are to refrain from engaging in work or activities that hinder the worship owed to God" (CCC 2185).

2. Uncle Les makes the argument that Christ is the only mediator we should ever use when praying, based on the Bible. (p.41-45) Do you think Uncle Les ever uses any other mediator (or intercessor) in his own prayer life?

   Virtually all Christians do. Anytime one asks another to pray for him he is asking for intercession. St. Paul told us to pray for one another. (See 1 Tim 2:1-3 and 2 Cor 1:11.)

3. Uncle Les also condemns idolatry. (p.42-43) Does he believe that Catholics are guilty of this sin, and why? Do you think that Uncle Les has a good understanding of Catholic Church teachings? How might you defend our use of statues of Jesus, the Blessed Mother, and the saints in our homes and churches?

   Les, like many Protestants, misunderstands Church teaching. We do not worship statues. The Church teaches that only God is to be worshipped. We use statues to call to mind the holy people they represent. Focusing on these holy people and modeling our lives after theirs helps us to be better Christians.

4. How is the method Uncle Les uses to interpret Scripture different from what you are used to? Whose interpretation does Uncle Les use? When you hear a priest talk about the meaning of a Scripture passage, whose interpretation is it? What happens when individuals interpret Scripture on their own?

Uncle Les relies strictly on his own interpretation. Catholics, on the other hand, have several wonderful sources of assistance. We have Sacred Tradition, which gives us the Church's interpretation passed down from the first centuries, we have the Magisterium of the Church, led by the Holy Spirit, and we have the work of countless faithful theologians over the centuries.

As Catholics, we can also use our own intellect and reasoning to interpret Bible passages, as long as our interpretations don't conflict with Church doctrine. But, solely relying on our own judgment would leave us open to error and is dangerous to our spiritual well-being. Speaking of the Epistles, St. Peter said, "In them there are some things hard to understand that the ignorant and unstable distort to their own destruction, just as they do the other Scriptures" (2 Pet 3:16).

5. Michael asks Uncle Les why Jesus chose twelve apostles. What is Les's answer? (p.46-48). Does this response really answer Michael's question? Is there another level of meaning, another interpretation?

The Twelve Apostles are symbolic of the twelve tribes of Israel — the tribes of the sons of Jacob. Les doesn't answer Michael's question fully, though. By gathering Twelve Apostles, Jesus signifies that he is beginning to re-establish Israel in fulfillment of prophecy. It is also significant that he chooses these Apostles to preach and teach. Why didn't he just write a guidebook — the New Testament — and tell his Apostles to help distribute it? Wouldn't that have been more efficient? The point is that from the beginning of human history, God has taught through word of mouth, by individuals.

Today the visible Church, built atop the structure of the first twelve bishops, continues to teach her people, rather than just handing out Bibles for people to interpret on their own.

6. Tammy remembers hearing about "old" South Philly (pre-air conditioning). (p.49-50) Can there be significant unintended consequences with the employment of new technology?

   Yes, and there are myriad examples. Cars, which provide us the opportunity to travel so quickly, kill many people. The telephone enables us to communicate from a distance and the result is that the intimacy of face-to-face communication is diminished. Refrigerated trucks enable us to eat fresh meat and produce from distant regions, which contributes to the radical re-structuring of local economies.

   Of course, new technology has some tremendous benefits as well, but we must be mindful of the proper order of things. Does a given innovation help us to achieve our goal eternity with God? It is most often not a question of whether to adopt a new gadget but rather a realization that we should let nothing interfere with what is most important in life.

7. There is a great snake in the dungeon of Michael's dream. (p.56-59) Does the serpent of Genesis 3:1-7 (the same as the one in Revelation 12:1-5) still exist, or is Satan merely a symbolic device? What does the Church teach about Satan?

   Satan exists. He is not some creation of the imagination that ancient people use to explain evil. (See CCC 391-398.)

8. Uncle Les's homily is very unsettling for Michael. (p.55-56) Why? Uncle Les seems to be quite an authority on Scripture. Confronted with Uncle Les's knowledge and apparent certainty about his biblical interpretations, might it be easy to start thinking that he is right? If you were in Michael's position, facing a conflict between the faith you love and a person you love, how might you react?

   Satan is the father of all lies. In Chapter 4 of Matthew's Gospel, Satan tempts Christ in the desert. Notice that Satan uses Scripture to try to trip up Christ. How easy for us to be deceived if we rely on our own understanding!

With regard to deciding between the love of a person and one's faith, understand that it is a false choice. The truth is still the truth even if you turn away from it. True love would never abandon the truth, but would hold fast to it. Even if the person we love does not recognize the truth, our turning away from it would certainly not help the situation!

Chapter 4

1. Uncle Les spends time teaching and working with his son and nephew. Michael notes that Elijah is more a junior partner than an employee or just a helper. (p.70) Does that strengthen the family bond?

   Working and learning together, whether through a family business, a family project, home schooling, or any other cooperative family venture, are powerful ways to strengthen family bonds, if done in love. Children can and should take on gradually increasing responsibilities through interaction with their parents.

2. Uncle Les talks about the distinct roles of men and women among the Amish. Are gender roles simply a function of culture? What does the Bible have to say about the roles of men and women? What does the Church say?

   Read 1 Cor 11:3 and Eph 5:21-33. Then read and consider the following Catechism passages: 369-373, 1577, and 2333-2335. There is often fierce debate about whether St. Paul was speaking only about the culture of the time (as with his requirement that women wear head coverings), or whether his view of husbands and wives is more deeply universal. These passages should provide plenty of grist for discussion!

3. Is Father Bucham a typical priest, in your experience? (p.73-77) Will a bearer of the truth always be well liked? What can we do to

help and encourage priests?

In my own experience, there are many priests like Fr. Bucham. No doubt, the bearer of the truth will not endear himself to everyone. There is something very attractive about the truth and many will hear it and respond, but others are not interested in the truth. Some do not really believe in the concept of truth, that there are absolutes. Others will not want to amend their ways to conform to God's will.

We need to be docile and submissive to the authority of the Church. We need to pray for our priests. This will encourage priests who often are too timid to preach the hard truths.

4. At the singing get-together, George talks about the mystery of suffering, and why some suffer while others seem not to. (p.79-80) Can God speak to us through a tiny bull-calf?

Yes, of course. God reveals himself through natural revelation and supernatural revelation. He is the author of nature and nature's laws. God can speak to us through a bull calf in the sense that we can observe a natural occurrence, reflect on it and gain insight and understanding.

5. George speaks of the importance of getting together to encourage and support one another. (p.80) Is there a biblical basis for this? What can we do in our own parishes to accomplish this objective?

The Bible instructs us to "rouse one another to love and good works. We should not stay away from the assembly, as is the custom of some, but encourage one another" (Heb 10:24-25). In our own parishes, we can be active in the various ministries and prayer groups already established, or work towards creating new ones if our parish is not an active one. We can reach out to new families in the parish, and offer help to those in need.

6. Les explains his evolution as a Christian. (p.83-86) If the Bible is the sole authority and individuals are to interpret it as best they can, what is likely to happen? Can sincere people come to believe in opposing doctrines, based on their own interpretations of the Bible?

It is likely that one's doctrinal beliefs, if unguided, will evolve over time. That would suggest that the truth is changeable and undergoes constant evolution, which is a contradiction. Sincere and devout people do come to various and contradictory beliefs, which they all believe are based on Scripture, but this is not the unity that Christ intended! As evidence of these many interpretations, consider the myriad Christian denominations that exist.

7. Who participated at the Council of Jerusalem in early Church history? (p.86-87) Did those present represent the leadership of the Church at this time? After the debate was finished, who "settled the matter"? What was James's role?

    Read Acts 15 up through (and especially) verse six: The apostles and elders — who represented the Church leadership — were gathered to consider whether circumcision was necessary for Gentile believers. After debate, it was Peter who rose and made a definitive decision (Acts 15:7-11). His statement ended the debate (Acts 15:12). Afterwards, James (the bishop of Jerusalem) added some relevant pastoral considerations.

8. Les charges that Catholics (and most Protestants) place the traditions of man on the same level as the Word of God. (p.85) What's wrong with this claim?

    The fact is, Sacred Scripture is only part of God's Word. St. Paul enjoins us to follow both what is written down and what is passed on by word of mouth, which is what the Church refers to as "Sacred Tradition." This is distinct from human tradition, which indeed should not take precedence over God's Word.
    (See 2 Thessalonians 2:15 and 1 Corinthians 11:2.)

9. What does the Church have to say about tobacco?

    Avoid excess, whether in food, tobacco, or alcohol.
    (See CCC 2290)

Chapter 5

1. How does the passage from 1 Corinthians 11: 27-29 read by Michael reinforce the belief in the Real Presence? (P.91)

    St. Paul is rebuking his audience for not showing the proper reverence when they take part in the Lord's Supper. Verse 29 warns those who partake but "do not discern the body," that they are eating and drinking judgment on themselves. This is strong and dramatic language. It shows that those not recognizing Holy Communion as truly the Body and Blood of Christ are partaking sacrilegiously.

2. What do you think is going through Michael's head, as he considers the Catholic versus Protestant interpretation of the 1 Corinthians passage? (p.91) How strong does his faith seem to you? How strong might it seem to Uncle Les? If you were in Michael's position, what might you do to gain some confidence in these situations?

    It is likely that Michael is anxious about what should be believed. It may be "easier" to believe that the Lord's Supper is just a symbolic re-enactment. It is difficult to determine how strong another's faith is. Michael admits doubt about the True Presence, but what he means is that he cannot comprehend the mystery of transubstantiation. That's understandable. It's no easier to comprehend than the mystery of the Incarnation — God becoming man in Jesus — yet all Christians believe that. In order to gain confidence and to strengthen faith it is necessary to study the Faith, including Scripture and Church history, especially the writings of the early Church Fathers. Prayer, meditation, and contemplation should complement one's study.

3. Jesus promised that the Holy Spirit would guide us to all truth. (p.93) Did he mean that all individuals seeking the truth prayerfully could derive it simply by praying to the Holy Spirit? Did he mean that a group of sincere people studying the Bible together would arrive at the truth? Does the Holy Spirit lead some to truth and others to confusion? Why do sincere Christians have so much difficulty agreeing on what the Bible teaches?

Read John 16:12-15. Jesus is addressing the apostles, the first bishops of the Church. Most Protestants take this passage out of context. They think it means that each individual Christian will be led to all truth. However, we know this can't be true because God is all Truth — He simply cannot guide some Christians to one truth and some to another. When people think they alone can discern the truth — apart from any guidance from God's Church, they are opening themselves up to pride and the guidance of Satan. Consider the passage about the Ethiopian eunuch (Acts 8:26-40). He tried to study Scripture on his own, but realized that without someone telling him what it said, he would not be able to understand it correctly.

4. Uncle Les implicitly criticizes both the plain people and the Catholic Church for practicing "shunning" or excommunication. (p.93) How would you respond to his criticism?

    Read Matthew 18:10-22 and CCC 1463: Jesus is directing the apostles on when to shun or excommunicate. Notice that Jesus instructs Peter to forgive often, seventy times seven, but that should not be confused with tolerating sin. Read Acts 5:1-11 for an example of how pre-meditated sin among those claiming to be Christian was not acceptable.

    St. Paul also tells Christians not to associate with fellow Christians who persist in sinful conduct (1 Cor 5:11). It may be helpful to reflect on or discuss to what extent individuals should "shun" persistent sinners, and to what extent this should be left to Church authorities. There is a delicate balance between being charitable to others in our thoughts and deeds and the need for us to avoid occasions of sin by associating with sinful people.

5. Uncle Les's homily brings up the "tobacco issue." (p.92-92) Can you pin point the areas in which Uncle Les's comments about church leadership and decision-making are clearly anti-Catholic? What aspects of the Church is Uncle Les disputing?

    Allegations: 1) Les claims that the Church leadership makes arbitrary decisions based on how such decisions will affect fund-raising. The leadership then imposes their decisions, regardless of what the Bible teaches. 2) Les claims that Church members who disagree with the decisions imposed by the leadership are simply excommunicated. 3) Les claims that a "tradition of man" puts the Bishop of Rome (the Pope) at the head of the Church. These are all false perceptions of the Catholic Church.

Responses: 1) Doctrinal decisions in the Church are made by the Bishops in conjunction with the Holy Father, and are based on the Word of God, both through Sacred Scripture and the Sacred Tradition handed down from the Apostles. 2) Excommunication in the Catholic Church is rare, even when members sometimes disagree both vehemently and openly with doctrine. This should impress us with the gravity of this discipline. 3) Jesus Christ is the Head of the Church, and the Pope his earthly Prime Minister. The Pope defends, protects, and promotes the deposit of faith. He doesn't decide what the deposit of faith is. (See later chapters for more detail on these issues.)

6. At this point in the story (p.94), do you see any change in the way Michael is thinking about Uncle Les and his preaching? Of all the questions running through Michael's head during this period, name the one that piqued your curiosity the most, and explain why.

Michael is still impressed with his uncle's sermons but less in awe. He has begun to question the accuracy of some of what his uncle has claimed. He is aware that Uncle Les is not appreciating some of the subtleties and nuances that are crucial for understanding.

Let me suggest two things Michael is considering: He is realizing that it doesn't make sense that the Holy Spirit, who leads us to all truth, could be the source of Protestantism's utter confusion, with all its competing and contradictory claims. If those outside the Catholic Church spoke with a unified voice that derived from a unified understanding of Scripture and doctrine it would be highly remarkable. The truth is, though, that they do not. Second, this is the first time Michael detects a less than charitable approach from his uncle. This should impress us with the importance of being charitable when we counter the false teachings of other Christians.

7. Was the Gospel of Matthew written for a Jewish audience? How can

you tell? (p.95-96)

*Yes. The term and prophecy of the Messiah originated in the
Jewish Scriptures, the Old Testament. The genealogy of Jesus was
given (in the beginning of Matthew's Gospel) so that the Jews could
see for themselves that Scripture had been fulfilled, that the
Messiah was in the line of Judah, a son of David.*

8. Luther questions how people could believe Peter was the leader of
   the early Church. (p.102-103) Why? Consider the passage in
   Galatians in which Paul rebukes Peter. How can this passage be
   reconciled with the doctrine of infallibility?

   *The Gospels provide examples in which Peter stumbles. He tries to
   protect Jesus from the Passion, indicating a profound lack of understanding about Christ's mission. He denies Christ three times in the
   courtyard. He is not even present for the Crucifixion.*

   *Then later, in Acts, we see a transformed Peter, a courageous leader,
   yet he is still rebuked by Paul. Read Galatians 2:11. It had been
   decided by Peter at the Council of Jerusalem that the Gentile
   Christians did not have to be circumcised or keep the Mosaic Law,
   that they were every bit as Christian as the Jews who had accepted
   Jesus as the Messiah. Peter was eating and associating with the
   Gentile converts, but when James came with many of the Jewish converts, Peter withdrew from the Gentiles for fear of offending the
   Jews. (Keep in mind that devout Jews did not associate with
   Gentiles.) Remember that Peter had been the one who had determined that there was now no difference between Gentile and Jew
   believers, but it was taking time for this teaching to take root.
   There was likely still tension and discomfort on both sides. Paul
   rebukes Peter precisely because he was not practicing what he
   preached, what he had decided and taught guided by the Holy
   Spirit at the Council of Jerusalem. So we see that Peter's teaching
   was correct and infallible, but his practice was in error. This passage thus supports the dogma of infallibility.*

9. Where did we get the Bible? (p.105-107) Does the answer have any
   implications for how it should be interpreted?

The Councils of Hippo and Carthage at the end of the fourth century determined which books of the New Testament were inspired. The work of the Councils was confirmed by the bishop of Rome, the Pope, and thereby was bound for all believers.

Protestants completely accept the Catholic Church's decision about which books are inspired and thus belong in the New Testament and which do not. At the same time, they reject the notion that the Holy Spirit leads the Catholic Church to all truth. How can these two points be reconciled? This is a dilemma for Protestants. Did the Church just happen to get it right about what should and shouldn't be included in the Bible? Could the Catholic Church have made a mistake? If so, then Protestants have to acknowledge that they do not have all the inspired words or that they have some books in the Bible that are not inspired. With regard to interpretation, one would have to admit that if the Holy Spirit led the Church to determine what should be included in Scripture, then it is only reasonable that the Holy Spirit still leads the same body to interpret it correctly.

10. Have you been "born again"? What does the term mean? (p.110)

Many Protestants use this term to mean "being saved" — accepting Jesus Christ as one's Lord and Savior. Read John Chapter 3: Jesus is showing that to be "born again" means to be baptized. Jesus is teaching Nicodemus about baptism in this chapter, and then later He instructs his disciples to baptize others under His authority.

11. Are we saved by faith alone? (p.111)

No. Romans 3:28 is the verse that many Protestants quote when asserting that we are saved by faith alone. However, "works of the law" in that passage does not refer to good deeds but rather to adherence to the Mosaic Law. What St. Paul is saying is that the Mosaic Law does not save us. Moreover, St. James explicitly states that "faith of itself, if it does not have good works, is dead" (Jam 2:17), and also, "See how a person is justified by works and not by faith alone" (Jam 2:24). In these passages, St. James is specifically referring to charitable works, which are necessary.

12. Contrast the popular and successful televangelists with the Missionaries of Charity. What is a Catholic hero? (p.113)

Televangelists preach and raise money to expand their operations. The Missionaries of Charity are not preachers. They are religious sisters, founded by Mother Teresa, who take vows of poverty, chastity, and obedience. They also take a vow of free service to the poorest of the poor. There is nothing wrong with preaching. Some are gifted and therefore called to it. St. Paul tells us that there are different gifts but the same Spirit (1 Cor 12:4).

What is worth mentioning is that many preachers throughout history have led people astray. They develop and even encourage such a devoted following themselves that they fail to lead people to Christ and the truth of the Gospel. St. Paul warned the early Christians often about false teachers.

Most Protestant ministers serve at the pleasure of their congregations, which tends to reinforce this problem. It can be difficult to preach hard truths to your congregation if you are constantly aware that they have the power to remove you. This is one of the reasons behind priests being rotated at parishes, to avoid a priest developing a following.

We must acknowledge that priests sometimes fail to preach hard truths and there are and have always been some who are "wolves in sheep's clothing." That's why it is important to know the Faith.

Chapter 6

1. Uncle Les and the young men make a trip to the feed mill to grind corn. (p.119-129) Les makes a number of observations about the "costs" of economic growth. (p.123-125) Does growth always equal progress? Why or why not? Can we learn something from the plain people?

Economic growth may equal progress from a secular humanist's

point of view. From the Christian point of view, growth is not nec-
essarily either good or bad. You can live the Gospel in a developing
country just as well as in an industrialized country. The book tries
to illustrate through Les that people tend to take the view that
growth is always and everywhere good. There are many pitfalls for
those who rely too heavily on technological progress and for those
who think the solution to all problems can be found if only we have
a big enough budget. Many plain communities have avoided the
myriad problems plaguing society in recent time — disrespect for
human life, family breakup, and tension between children and their
parents — but have done it through their culture and the upbring-
ing of their children, not with costly social programs.

2. The tobacco issue is discussed at a special meeting at Uncle Les's
    church (p.132-141) What point does this discussion illustrate about
    the difficulties inherent with Bible-only Christianity? (p.135)

    The Bible has nothing explicit to say about tobacco growing and its
    use. Therefore people of good will can (and do!) come to contra-
    dictory conclusions if forced to determine what a Christian's pos-
    ture should be with regard to this issue. Again, if every person is
    his own authority you will necessarily have disunity. There is also
    the potential problem of wrongly elevating what is more of a cultur-
    al issue (e.g., growing and using tobacco) into the status of a doc-
    trine.

3. Uncle Les's church might split because of the tobacco issue. (p.142)
    Michael tells Eli that that would never happen in a Catholic parish,
    because Catholics don't disagree about doctrine. What exactly is
    "doctrine," and why don't Catholics split over disagreements about
    doctrine?

    Doctrines are the unchanging truths taught by the Church. To be a
    Catholic means to believe in the infallibility of the teaching author-
    ity of the Church in matters of faith and morals. God's Truth,
    entrusted to the Church, is unchanging. Therefore, for Catholics to
    disagree on doctrinal matters would entail disbelieving the basis of
    the Church itself. Remember, though, that there are many non-doc-
    trinal areas in which Catholics may express sincere disagreement
    — for example, whether capital punishment should be allowed.

Also, some Catholics do express disagreement over doctrines. Some leave the Church, while others remain, despite their disagreements.

Chapter 7

1. On pages 146-147, Michael explains the teaching authority of the Catholic Church to Eli. Why do you think this is so difficult for Eli to understand?

   This is a foreign concept for Eli. If anything unites Bible-only Christians, it is their search for truth according to individual interpretation of Scripture. In their minds, no church can "tell you" what to believe, because they allow no place for the oral Word of God passed down from the Apostles (which we call Sacred Tradition).

2. Where in the Bible is Peter called to be the leader of the Church (the Pope)? (p.148)

   Read Matthew 16:13-20 and John 21:15-19. The most critical part is where Peter is given the "keys of the kingdom," which were not given to any other disciple. The keys confer on Peter the office of "Prime Minister" to Christ the King. He is given the authority to "bind and loose," and whatever he declares bound on earth, is bound in heaven. Since we know that no falsehood can exist in heaven, it must mean that Peter can declare no false doctrine on earth. This is Christ's promise of infallibility to Peter and all the successive popes.

3. Eli scoffs at the whole concept of infallibility. (p.148-149) Explain what "infallibility" does and does not mean. Why does Eli take issue with the idea that Peter was called by Christ to lead the Church?

   Infallibility means judging the truth in all matters of doctrine. It does not mean that the Pope never sins (that would be "impeccability"). It does not mean that the Pope never says anything that is incorrect, or that he is an expert on scientific matters. Eli has a problem with Peter leading the Church precisely because Peter is a sinner. But, as we know, all of us are sinners, even the highest leaders of the Church.

4. Eli asks Michael if he believes that Peter was the leader of the apostles and was infallible. Michael answers yes, but does not explain the doctrine of infallibility to Eli or correct Eli's misconceptions. (p.148) In what ways does Michael's lack of response hinder Eli's understanding of these issues?

    Because of Michael's inability to provide an explanation, Eli will continue to misunderstand the doctrine of infallibility. He may assume that since no explanation is attempted, there probably is none. In situations like this, it would be better to indicate that there is an answer, and to own up to the fact that you're unable to explain it adequately without studying it further. Then, always follow up with the person.

5. Describe the Dominican order. (p.149-150) Who founded the order? What is unique about the origin of the Dominican order?

    St. Dominic founded the order in the thirteenth century. The Order of Preachers (OP) fanned out across Europe to defend the faith against the false teachings of the Albigensians.

6. What is God's promise to those who respond to the call to religious life? (P.150)

    Retirement benefits that are "out of this world!" Read Matthew 19:27-30.

7. What are the three categories of eunuchs identified by Christ? (P.151)

    See Matthew 19:12. Some men are eunuchs from birth — unable to procreate due to some naturally occurring condition. Others are castrated by their captors. The third category that Jesus speaks of are those who make themselves eunuchs "for the sake of the kingdom." Read page 151 for an explanation.

8. Michael reads a tract his uncle gives him about the Inquisition. (p.154-155) Why is it so easy for Michael to believe what he reads? What dilemma does the Inquisition pose for Michael?

It's easy for him to believe anything about the Inquisition because he's never read any facts on the subject from a Catholic source. He's unprepared to dispute the information from his uncle, and if he believes it, then he wonders how he can be a part of a Church that participated in these seeming atrocities.

This incident represents a key problem for so many Catholics. Many are drawn away from the Church when they are presented with attacks on Catholic doctrine or stories of Catholics behaving in an un-Christian fashion. Because they have little knowledge about what the Church teaches and why, they become easy prey to whatever denomination is making the one-sided presentation. Catholics need to equip themselves with a thorough knowledge of both the Bible and the Catholic Catechism in order to refute these claims.

9. Contrast the convent with Les's church. (p.156, 159-160). Does the artwork detract from or aid worship to God?

Les's church is plain and austere. It contains no artwork, no altar, and no statues. The convent, on the other hand, is replete with tapestries, artwork, and statues, and has an altar in the chapel. It is beautiful to behold. This beauty is meant to magnify the glory of God, not to detract from it. God reaches out through time and matter. The matter that we surround ourselves with should help us focus on God.

Imagine you had appointments to see two different kings. As you walk toward the throne of the first one, you notice that the walls are bare. The floor is bare. When you reach the king, he is sitting on a plain stool by himself. As you walk toward the second king, the hallway is adorned with art on the walls, a beautiful carpet, and chandeliers hang from the ceiling. His throne is splendid and his queen and an entire court accompany him. Which kingdom is more impressive? Do the artwork, carpets, beauty of the throne, and the court detract from the king's glory or magnify the king's glory?

10. Describe what Michael is experiencing as he gazes at a relief of the Crucifixion in the convent chapel. (p.157) He wonders whether witnessing the Crucifixion in person would have helped him in his doubt. Do you think it would have? Why or why not?

Michael thinks that if he were physically present for the Crucifixion, he could evaluate Christ for himself and know more certainly who He was and what He intended for mankind. But, many (if not most) of those present for the Crucifixion continued to doubt that Christ was our Savior. The fact that He suffered and died, rather than being "saved" by God reaffirmed his status as a failure to those witnessing the event.

11. Tammy offers up her suffering for those who suffer for the Faith. (p.160) What does the Church teach about offering up suffering, and uniting our pain or grief with the suffering of Christ?

Suffering is "a participation in the saving work of Jesus." (See CCC 1508 and 1521, and also 2 Cor 12:9 and Col 1:24.) By offering up our own sufferings, we can aid other suffering souls, including those in purgatory.

12. Does Satan harm us directly? (p.161) How does he work?

Satan very rarely is able to harm us directly. But, by subtly influencing our thoughts and emotions, he can wreak even greater harm. (See CCC 395.)

Chapter 8

1. On page 165, Michael remembers the "mystical insight" that he had the night before. What is that insight? (p.157-159) Why is he remembering it all now at this part of the Mass?

The "insight" is that the Eucharist is the re-presentation of Christ's sacrifice on Calvary. Jesus is truly present in the Eucharist as he was on the cross. Michael remembers this insight as he approaches to receive the Eucharist. It is extra-ordinary in itself that the sacrifice of Christ can be made present to us, but even more awesome is the invitation extended to us to partake, to eat His Flesh and drink His Blood. This is what He commanded. This is how spiritual kinship is possible, how we become sons and daughters of God the Father and brothers and sisters to our brother Jesus. It is a bond that transcends time, culture, and place.

2. Do you think Michael's experiences with the Bible-only Christians in Kentucky have had an impact on his thinking? Would he likely be having the same thoughts and ideas if he were still in Philadelphia, going through his normal routine? Have you ever had an experience that suddenly opened your eyes to a discovery about your faith?

   Conflicting ideas can be great aids to understanding. The challenges to the faith forced Michael to grow, to learn and consider things that can at times be taken for granted. I learned much more about Catholicism at Temple University, a secular college, than at Villanova, a Catholic one, even though I took three theology courses at Villanova and only economics at Temple. At Temple I was challenged to defend what the Church teaches on such issues as abortion and homosexuality. At Villanova it was much less likely that those issues would even come up in conversation.

3. What does the Church teach about the substance of the Eucharist? Is it a symbol, or something more? (p.166)

   Read CCC 1373-1377 (especially paragraph 1374). Christ is truly present, under the appearance of bread and wine. This means that at the consecration, though the substance still looks and tastes like bread and wine, it is not. It is Jesus Christ.

4. On page 167, Uncle Les is thinking about what is happening on Michael's "road to conversion and accepting Christ as his personal Lord and Savior." What does he mean by that? Do you think Michael's relationship with Our Lord would be different if he were a Protestant? In what ways?

   Les believes that Michael cannot "accept Jesus Christ" without leaving the Catholic Church. The Church, to Les's mind, is con-

trary to God's Word and therefore it would be a contradiction to be a Catholic and accept Jesus Christ. The Catholic Church asserts many things that are condemned by non-Catholic Christians: that the Catholic Church is the One, True Church, that Jesus is present in the Eucharist, that Christ forgives sins through his priests, that the pope is the earthly leader of the Church, and many more.

There is a distinction between Protestants and Catholics with respect to their relationship with Jesus. While both may seek Jesus in personal prayers of praise, thanksgiving, and petition, only Catholics have the ultimate personal relationship with Jesus — physical and spiritual communion with Him through the Holy Eucharist.

5. Are Catholics "Christians"? (p.169) Why do some Protestants claim that they are not? How would you answer a charge by some one that you are not a Christian?

Yes! Of course Catholics are Christians. Many Protestants would deny that because they perceive that the Catholic Church teaches beliefs handed down through Sacred Tradition, in addition to Sacred Scripture. If someone says or implies that you are not a Christian, I would press them to explain why they think that. Then state simply that you believe in Jesus Christ, the only Son of God, Who was conceived by the Holy Spirit, born of the Virgin Mary, and Who suffered and died to save us from our sins. That pretty much sums up the definition of a Christian.

6. Discuss the Inquisition. Do sins committed by individual Catholics or groups of Catholics tell us anything about whether or not what the Catholic Church teaches is true? (p.171-174) Michael makes the point that "the truth is the truth even if all the followers are not very good at following it, or even if there are no followers at all." (p.173) What is he trying to say?

The book discusses the Inquisition briefly. There is a tremendous amount of misinformation, misunderstanding, and exaggeration about the events referred to as the Inquisition. The important point is that it is often invoked by both Protestants and secularists in an attempt to discredit the Church. It does nothing of the sort. A sin-

ner does not discredit the teachings of the Church any more than a car thief discredits the Constitution of the United States. Indeed, you can call something a sin precisely because the Church teaches us what is sinful.

Sin can cause serious scandal. (Read CCC 2284, 2285, and 2286, then read Matthew 18:6, Luke 17:1, and 1 Cor 8:10-13.) Scandal is a grave sin and is even more dangerous for those in positions of authority. When one's sins lead others to sin it is a tragedy, but the reality of scandal does not undermine the truth. Whether the teachings of the Catholic Church are the truth or not does not depend on the behavior of any members in the Church. For example, a priest's hypocrisy (sinfulness) can lead others to sin, but does not have any effect whatsoever on the teaching authority of the Church.

In the course of salvation history, the Jews sinned against God in many scandalous ways, yet God kept His covenant with them. Also, Christ calls the scribes and Pharisees "hypocrites," yet he admonishes the Jews to "do and observe all things whatsoever they tell you," because these officials validly have taken their seat on "the chair of Moses." (Matt 23:1-3). He is saying that these officials possessed valid authority from God, even if they did not live up to what they taught.

Saying that the truth is the truth regardless of what people may believe is affirming the notion of moral absolutes. Moral relativists believe that the "truth" depends on what people happen to believe, that there is no absolute truth. Read John 18:33-38. Pilate mocks the notion that there is a "truth." Could this be why Pilate did not resist the Jews who wanted Jesus crucified? Pilate knew Jesus was not guilty, but he gave in to the will of the crowd. For Pilate, the "truth" was that the people wanted Him crucified. This concept of whether truth is absolute or relative has profound implications. A relativist may insist that abortion, homosexuality, or slavery are not inherently wrong. An absolutist (a Catholic one) knows that all these things are wrong even if — at times — the vast majority of people disagree.

7. Michael refers to the parable of the farmer sowing wheat when explaining why the Inquisition is not proof that the Catholic Church

is not the True Church. (p.174) How would you explain this to someone new to the subject? Who is the wheat? The weeds? Where do the wheat and weeds ultimately end up?

The wheat represents good people, and the weeds, evil people. The wheat is taken to the master's barn, which symbolizes heaven. The weeds are burned — hell! Jesus was also making the point to the apostles that it is not man's job to judge (that is, to separate the wheat from the weeds), but only God's. (We can and should, however, make judgments about particular actions or behaviors — for example, we should judge that lying is wrong or stealing is wrong.)

8. Pam has seen "far more souls become entrenched through argument than moved." (p.179) Is there something to be learned here?

Yes, there is a great practical lesson. When defending the Faith keep your ultimate goal in mind. You are trying to win a soul, not an argument. If you are focused on winning the argument you are doing so for your own sake. It is prideful. In trying to win a soul, on the other hand, you are concerned with the other's well-being and eternal destiny. Be charitable. Love the person even when he is being defensive and inaccurate. Focus not on an argument but on presenting the truth in love.

Chapter 9

1. What is Luther's objection to Michael's using sources other than the Bible to support the Catholic position on the papacy? (p.183-184) Is Luther's analogy about the glasses of water fair? Why or why not?

The Bible, says Luther, is inspired and without error. Other sources are not. Why consult sources that you are unsure about when trying to find the truth? His analogy is actually a good argument against the Protestant doctrine of Sola Scriptura (the Scriptures alone). How would one know which glass of water was clean and pure? With water, it is not always obvious when it is tainted. You would have to trust someone who checked all the water glasses and

determined that one was pure. Similarly, one's belief in the "pure-
ness" of the Bible presumes faith in the Church that compiled it.

I've heard some insist that God used the Catholic Church as an
instrument to produce the Bible, but that the Church is still apos-
tate. That idea is preposterous — that the Church was led by the
Holy Spirit to compile the inspired Scriptures, but was then misled
about other matters of faith.

2. Luther quotes 2 Timothy 3:16 in saying that: "All Scripture is given by inspiration by God, that the man of God may be complete, thorough-ly equipped for every good work." (p.185) Does this mean that we need only the Bible to follow what God wants us to do in our lives?

No. St. Paul is saying that if you want to be a complete man of
God, the Scriptures are a useful and profitable tool. But, nowhere
does he say that the Scriptures alone are sufficient for becoming
complete. Think about an army providing a man with a uniform,
gun, and mess kit to equip him to be a soldier. These things would
certainly be useful to him, but in no way sufficient. The man would
still need officers to train him and command him, and fellow sol-
diers to fight with him. If he were left on his own with just his
equipment, he would be highly ineffective! Just so, we need more
than a Bible in our hands — we need the Church!

3. Present the "rock" argument that supports the Catholic position for the papacy. (p.186-190)

Christ spoke Aramaic with fellow Jews. The New Testament, however,
was originally written in Greek. "Petros" (the Greek masculine word
for "rock") means small stone, and "Petra" (the feminine from)
means large boulder. Christ says, "Blessed are you, Simon bar Jona!
you shall be called Rock" (translations differ: some say, "you shall be
called Peter"). The word in Aramaic for stone, large or small, is
Kepha, but when this exchange was written in Greek there arose the
Petra-Petros translation problem. It would have been silly to change
Simon's name to Petra, a female name. The other point is that gram-
matically speaking, rock clearly refers to Peter himself, not to Peter's
confession of Jesus being the Messiah.
The "rock" argument, though, is not as crucial in establishing

Peter's primacy as Matthew 16:19, "I will give you (singular in the Greek) the keys to the kingdom."

4. Explain what events are being foretold or described in Matthew Chapter 24. Why was the temple destroyed? (P.193)

   Read Matthew 24: Jesus prophesies about the siege of Jerusalem and the destruction of the Temple. This occurred in 70 AD, before "this generation passes" (verse 34). The Temple was no longer needed. It had served its purpose. Christ ascended into heaven and provided time for the Gospel to be preached "first to Judah and the lost sheep of Israel" — the Jews. Then came the destruction as Jesus had said it would. The Temple has never been rebuilt. The Jewish religion has not been practiced (no animal sacrifice, no ark of the covenant) as it was at the time of Christ, since the destruction of the Temple.

5. Michael tells Luther that he is not the one who originated the claim of Peter as the first pope. Where, then, did this claim originate? (P.194)

   That Peter was the first earthly leader of the Church is made clear in both Scripture and in Sacred Tradition. Peter was the bishop of Rome, where he was eventually martyred (although his martyrdom is not explicitly described in Scripture). Keep in mind that the Pope (this title, which just means "papa," came later) is the bishop of Rome. The office of Pope is sometimes referred to as the "Chair of Peter."

6. During the Bible study with Uncle Les and the members of his church, Michael starts to question their reliance on the Bible alone to solve every question. (p.195) He then explains to them that the Bible is not meant to be a catechism. What does he mean by that? Is it a good idea to use the Bible as a catechism? Why or why not?

   Read CCC 5: Catechesis is an education in the Faith. The Faith is more than what is contained in Scripture (See 2 Thes 1:15 and 3:6). Catechism originated in the first century when most people couldn't read, so instruction took place by the verbal recital of questions and answers. The books contained in the New Testament are not a catechism. They are the teachings of Jesus, plus information about where He went, whom He healed, and His death and resurrection, as well as the later epistles of Paul and others.

7. Describe the three-fold denial of Christ by Peter and then the later three-fold reconciliation between Christ and Peter. (p.198-200)

Read John 18:15-27 and then John 21:4-19. By a charcoal fire in the courtyard of the high priest, Peter denies that he is a follower of Christ three times just as Christ had prophesied. The risen Christ reconciles Himself to Peter on the shore of the sea of Tiberias. There He had a charcoal fire where they cooked their breakfast. Christ tells Peter to bring some of the fish and Peter hauls the net ashore. This is a foreshadowing of the Church. Peter was to "bring in" the catch. Notice that it is a large catch but that the net did not break. After breakfast, Christ asks Peter if he loves Him three times. Peter affirms — three times — that he does love Christ. (This particular Scripture passage can be studied in much greater depth with the aid of a good commentary.) He, Peter, is charged with the task of tending and feeding Jesus' flock.

8. To whom did Jesus entrust the "keys of the Kingdom"? Discuss the full significance of Matthew 16:19.

The keys are entrusted only to Peter (the "you" in verse 19 is singular in the Greek). The keys are a symbol of authority. Read Isaiah 22:21-22. Entrusting the key to Eliakim represented a transfer of authority in the Davidic kingdom.

Then read Revelation 1:18 and 3:7. Christ holds the key in heaven. In any kingdom the king has authority. He delegates authority to a cabinet of ministers. The Prime Minister, who holds the key, is given authority by the king to bind and loose, to determine obligations to the king and to dispense with obligations. In the Church, the bishops are Christ's "cabinet of ministers," and the pope is the "Prime Minister." Note that the pope cannot take anything away from the deposit of faith. By virtue of his office he is incapable of teaching error.

Chapter 10

1. Michael presents text from Jeremiah and 1 Kings to illustrate the custom of the "Gebirah" (Queen Mother). (p.221-223) Explain how these passages show that Catholics are correct in calling Mary our Queen.

    Jeremiah 13:18 and 1 Kings 2:12-20 provide biblical evidence for this accepted practice in the Davidic Kingdom. The mother of the king was the queen mother, who shared the throne. She had no power in her own right, but she had the king's ear, and Scripture shows that the king listened to his mother. The mother was the one to fulfill the role of queen because the king often had many wives. Christ, who came to re-establish the kingdom on a spiritual level, is the eternal King. He, too, has His mother in heaven who shares His throne. It is appropriate, then, that we view Mary the mother of Jesus as our Queen. We ask her to pray for us, for she is the most powerful intercessor.

2. In the Old Testament, what three items were contained in the Ark of the Covenant, and what did each of these represent? (p.224-225) In what ways is Christ the New Testament fulfillment of each of these? How, then, is Mary understood to be the Ark of the New Covenant?

    First, the Ten Commandments were given by God to Moses for the Israelites. An ark, a small but elaborate box (roughly two feet by three feet) was built to house the stone tablets. The Decalogue or Ten Commandments were literally the Word of God. Later, a jar of manna was placed in the Ark (Exodus 16), to remind the Israelites that God provided manna from heaven to sustain the Israelites as they wandered in the dessert. It was the "bread of life." The rod of Aaron was also included (Numbers 16 and 17). This was the rod that sprouted and thus revealed to the Israelites the true priesthood of Aaron and his descendents and the authority that went with the priesthood.

    Christ became the new and everlasting High Priest (Hebrews 2), thus fulfilling the rod of Aaron. The first chapter of the Gospel according to John says, "the Word became flesh," which shows how the Incarnation of Christ is a fulfillment of the tablets of God's Word. Then, in John 6, Christ refers to himself as the "bread of life," the fulfillment of the bread that sustained the Israelites who wandered in the desert. Since Christ fulfilled all that was in the ark, Mary was the fulfillment of the ark itself. She carried the contents of the Ark of the New Covenant — the body of the infant Jesus — within her body.

3. Review 2 Samuel 6:6-19 and Luke Chapter 1. What are the parallels between the Ark in the Old Testament and Mary as the Ark of the New Covenant? (p.227)

    David went before the ark and danced for joy. The infant, John the Baptist, leapt in his mother's (Elizabeth's) womb when Mary came to visit.

    David was in awe and humbly asked himself, "Who am I that the Ark of the Lord comes to me?" Elizabeth asked, "Who am I that the mother of my Lord should come to me?"

    The Ark stayed in the house of Obed-Edom for three months and Mary stayed with Elizabeth for three months.

4. Do Catholics worship Mary? (p.227) How might it appear that way to Protestants? How would you respond to someone making this charge against Catholics?

    Catholics do not worship Mary. We honor her and ask her to pray for us, to intercede with the King, Jesus. It can very well seem like worship to a non-Catholic observer. Because they don't believe in the communion of saints and that saints can intercede for us, they have no theology explaining the position and role of those in the Faith who have died and gone before us. It is simple enough to explain that we honor Mary, but do not worship her. This is a good opportunity to show a skeptic the Catechism of the Catholic Church. Show them that it forbids worship of Mary. This should impress any doubter that they are mistaken and might have other misconceptions as well. Let them know that the Catechism is an exhaustive resource available to anyone, Catholic or not.

5. Study the book of Revelation, from the end of Chapter 11 to the

beginning of Chapter 12. Who does the woman clothed with the sun represent? (p.228-229) In what way is this woman portrayed as the Ark of the New Covenant?

She represents Mary the mother of Jesus. She also is representative of Israel. At the very end of Revelation, Chapter 11, John sees God's temple in heaven. It is open and he can see the Ark of the Covenant that was in the Temple. Then, beginning in Chapter 12, the great sign is mentioned, the woman clothed with the sun. John goes right from seeing the Ark to seeing the woman. (Note that the designation of chapters and verses was not added to Scripture until after the first millennium.)

The Woman gives birth to a male child who "is to rule all the nations with an iron rod." That is taken directly from the book of Psalms. This child is Jesus. Keep in mind that this is the book of Revelation, in which things are "revealed" to us. The fact that Mary is the fulfillment of the Ark is just one of these revelations.

Chapter 11

1. Can one "will" another to the truth? Why or why not? (p.239)

    No. God created us with a free will. We cannot be forced to acknowledge and respond to the truth and neither can we force another to submit to the truth. We should not even attempt it. We are compelled to present the truth. From there it becomes a matter of whether the free will of the individual will cooperate with the grace of God.

2. Why do Protestants believe that the Bible is the inspired Word of God? (p.240) Are there any problems in the logic underlying their reasons?

    Practically speaking, they believe the Bible is inspired because they have been taught so, either from a young age or by the person who brought them to the Christian faith. Or, you can say that they accept the Bible because it is accepted by Christians to be the Word of God, that it is a consensus.

There are a few Scripture passages they might use to try to show that the Bible is God's Word. However, to use Scripture itself to prove the inspiration of Scripture begs the question. Any book could claim to be inspired. Have they read every book? How many claim to be inspired? If a book came out tomorrow that claimed to be inspired would you believe it to be inspired?

Second, if you were taught that something was inspired, that leads to the question of who taught your teacher and how can they be trusted? Indeed, who was the first to assert that the Bible was the inspired Word of God? Who determined which books should be in the Bible? The Catholic Church!

If you believe that the Bible is inspired, then you must believe that the Catholic Church was led by the Holy Spirit at least that one time when she correctly compiled the books of the New Testament.

3. Is having your faith challenged a good thing? Why or why not? (p.240)

Yes. Rejoice for the opportunity to spread the True Faith. If the challenger is less than cordial, then it can be a wonderful opportunity to practice humility. Act with charity and concern for the other person's soul. If you don't know something, don't be afraid to acknowledge that and thank them for challenging you with a good question.

4. Discuss how the act of providing an explanation of the Faith is as important as the explanation itself. (P.243)

If you do not speak with love and good will your posture will contradict the content of the Gospel. By uncharitable actions you will be providing a stumbling block for those who need to hear and respond. In other words, they will hear the Gospel, but experience something that is contrary to it and will be slow or reluctant to respond because of it.

When you explain and defend you are trying to win a soul, not an argument. Try not to become argumentative, but neither be without passion. It is appropriate to be zealous about the truth. It can be difficult to remain charitable at times and if you are ungracious, humble yourself and apologize.

Do not engage in discussion with those who ridicule and are not interested in the truth. Be as tolerant as possible but do not "cast your pearls before swine" (Matt 7:6).

5. Michael says that the Blessed Mother was "there" at all the important times. (p.246) Which times were they?

    She was there at the Annunciation and at the birth of Jesus. She carried Jesus to Egypt to escape Herod's persecution. She raised Jesus. She brought Jesus to the Temple for the Presentation. She found Jesus in the Temple teaching the elders when he was twelve years old. She prompted Jesus' first miracle at Cana. She was there when Jesus carried his cross to Calvary, when he was crucified, and taken down from the cross. She was there in Jerusalem with the disciples when the Holy Spirit descended on them on the feast of Pentecost.

6. What is meant by salvation history? (p.247)

    Salvation history is simply the story of how mankind (Adam and Eve) originally sinned against God, and how God promised to redeem mankind from this sin. It encompasses all of the words of the prophets foretelling the Messiah, the covenants God made with his people over time, and the eventual arrival of Jesus Christ and his saving death and resurrection.

7. Summarize the fall and redemption by comparing Adam's behavior with Christ's. (p.247-249) Then compare and contrast Eve's role with Mary's. (P.249-250)

    Read Genesis 2 and 3, and Mark 14 (the Agony in the Garden). Read Luke 1 (the Annunciation). Adam was charged with "keep- ing" the garden. He failed in his task. He allowed Eve to be deceived and then he too ate from the tree of the knowledge of good and evil. He was afraid of the serpent and failed to ask God for help. Sin entered the world.

Christ was sent to reconcile man with God. He too had a mission. When his hour came, he too was afraid and prayed that the cup might be taken away, if it was the will of the Father. In a garden, Gethsemane, Jesus prayed for the strength to do the will of the Father. God sent an angel to comfort him. The opportunity for communion with God became a reality.

An angel was sent to block the way to the Garden of Eden so that fruit from the "tree of life" could not be eaten. Christ crucified became the new "tree of life." His flesh, received in the Eucharist, is the fruit.

With regard to Eve and Mary, both acted as conduits. Through Eve's disobedience to God, sin and death entered the world. Through Mary's obedience to God, Jesus was born and died for us, resulting in reconciliation and eternal life.

Chapter 12

1. Compare and contrast the view of church authority held by Catholics and Amish versus the views of Bible-only believers. (p.254) What differences are there, if any, between Catholics and Amish with respect to their views of church authority?

   Catholics believe that the Church teaches with authority. That is, we are bound to believe what the Church teaches in the areas of faith and morals. We are also compelled to adhere to what the Church prescribes with regard to disciplines and practices, such as not eating meat on Fridays in Lent and participating at Mass on Sundays and Holy Days of obligation. When the Pope and bishops teach we are to listen, believe, and obey.

   The Amish are not universal in the sense that there is no papacy. The local bishops have authority and direct what is proper with regard to worship and practice in their local communities. There is no specifically Amish catechism. That is, the various churches do believe in the same fundamentals, but there are some differing doc-

trines among groups calling themselves Amish.

Bible-only Christians do not adhere to any authority other than the Bible, or more accurately, their interpretation of the Bible.

2.   Uncle Les claims that all churches are apostate in some way. What does he mean by this, and is it true? Why or why not?

Uncle Les means that all churches (denominations), because they are made up of men, have strayed to some extent. This understanding among many Bible-only Christians leads them to avoid any denomination and to even avoid any denominational identification. There is a desire not to get pre-occupied with doctrinal beliefs but with just being "a good Christian." There are many "non-denominational" Christian churches and even groups of Christians who choose to "home-church," who believe that they are avoiding the trap of defining themselves through their doctrinal beliefs. However, every one of these groups has a set of beliefs, or doctrines, determined by the pastor. When that pastor leaves their church, the new pastor will likely espouse at least some doctrines that are different from the preceding one.

All denominations founded by men are in error to some extent (the extent varies from denomination to denomination), but Christ founded His Church (Matthew 16:18) and Jesus promised that the Holy Spirit would lead the Church to all truth (John 16:12-13). Therefore, for a Christian to insist that all denominations are in error is unscriptural.

The Magisterium of the Church — the bishops in union with the Pope — is protected from teaching error. This does not mean that her members never teach falsely or never fail to live up to what the Church teaches. There have been and remain many false teachers and we all sin. This is not evidence that the Church teaches error.

What is also important to realize is the impossibility of "just being a Christian," free from all doctrinal considerations. To be a Christian means, in part, to believe certain things — for example, that Jesus is the Son of God. He was crucified, died, and was buried. He rose from the dead on the third day. But what else is a

sincere Christian to believe? Is it enough to believe the fundamen-
tals of Christianity? If so, what are the fundamentals? Who deter-
mines what a Christian is to believe? If someone insists that all
you need to believe as a Christian is X, Y, and Z, then they are pro-
viding a set of beliefs; they are establishing doctrine.

Typically, Bible-only Christians who attempt to promote the funda-
mentals of the faith are not escaping doctrinal considerations, only
trying to simplify them. In this way "non-denominationalists"
become a denomination unto themselves.

To illustrate, consider two Christians who begin a denomination.
They strive to adhere to the fundamentals of the Christian faith.
One believes in the Trinity while the other does not. (By the way,
the Trinity is not taught explicitly in Scripture.) They agree, for the
sake of unity, to leave that issue up to the individual believer. For
them, the Trinity becomes an issue that a Christian can believe but
need not. What they are saying is that such a belief is not "funda-
mental." What results with this approach is a set of core beliefs
that everyone happens to agree with. It serves to "pare down"
Christianity for the sake of doctrinal unity.

3. Michael is impressed with the honesty of the Amish during the auction.
   Discuss how an individual's actions can hurt or help the body of
   believers.

   Good actions build up the body of Christ while sinful actions cause
   harm. While we do not see the "ripple effect" of our actions, they
   are real. A dramatic example might be King Henry VIII's adultery
   with Anne Boleyn. This sin eventually led to Henry's desire to
   divorce his wife. When forbidden to do so by the Church a signifi-
   cant rupture was the result. Parliament appointed Henry the head
   of the Church in England and bloodshed and injustice ensued. Sin
   begets sin.

4. The contrast between the dress of the Amish and the "English" is
   striking. (p.259) What is each group trying to achieve with their
   dress? What do the Bible and the Catechism teach us about how
   Christians should dress?

The Amish dress "plainly." They wear basic colors of black, gray, dark blue, and white. The women do not wear jewelry or make-up. They dress "modestly" so as not to call attention to themselves. The effect is that they do draw attention to themselves outside their own circles because by today's standards their dress is very different.

Read CCC 2521 and 2522: "Purity requires modesty. Modesty is decency. It inspires one's choice of clothes." The Catholic Church does not offer specific guidelines with regard to dress, but rather seeks to make clear, in general terms, that a Christian ought to be mindful of what he or she wears in so far as it promotes the virtue of modesty.

5. Why does Michael prefer to be called "Catholic" as opposed to "Roman Catholic"? (P.261)

The modifier "Roman" came after the Church in England broke away. They came to be known as "Anglican" or "Anglican Catholic." To distinguish between the denominations the modifier "Roman" was used to describe those who remained loyal to the bishop of Rome, the pope, and the Magisterium (the teaching authority) of the Church. "Catholic" comes from a Greek word meaning universal. Michael prefers to consider that only one Church is truly universal. There is no great need to add any modifier.

There is often confusion when people talk about the Ukrainian Catholic Church or the Byzantine rite liturgy. These are in fact Catholics, in communion with Rome, who do not use the "Latin" rite liturgy, the liturgy with which the vast majority of American Catholics are familiar.

6. Is the Catholic Church "above the Bible" as Pastor Brown suggests to Michael? (p.261)

No. The Church fixed the canon of the Bible in the councils of Hippo and Carthage in the late fourth century. That is, Church authorities determined, with guidance from the Holy Spirit, which books belonged in the collection of books that came to be known as the Bible.

There are some Church teachings that may appear, at first glance, to contradict certain Bible verses. These are usually cases in which a passage needs to be read in the full context for proper understanding. For example, St. Paul writes that women should have their heads covered when in prayer. It is not a current rule or discipline of the Church, though, that women have their heads covered at Mass. Seem like a contradiction? Not at all. St. Paul made this ruling in a particular situation for a particular group of believers. It dealt with a practice or custom, rather than a matter of doctrine. It was binding and it was to be obeyed, but it was not a universal judgment meant to be binding for all believers for all time. (By the way, how many Protestants do you know who insist that women keep their heads covered during prayer? While fundamentalists are fond of pointing out verses in Scripture that appear to contradict Catholic teachings, the fact is that there are far more areas in which Protestant teachings disregard the direct words of Christ, especially with regard to such key doctrines as the Eucharist, the Papacy, and confession.)

7. In Matthew's Gospel, Chapter 23, Jesus explicitly says, "Call no man on earth your father." (p.263) By calling priests "father," aren't Catholics acting in direct contradiction of Christ's teaching? Explain.

    No, because this passage was not meant to be taken literally. The Church, who interprets Scripture authoritatively, has understood from apostolic times that Jesus was using hyperbole to make a point. The point was to be mindful of the source of all fatherhood, namely God the Father.

    Men are able to father children biologically only because we have been given the privilege to share in God's creation. Priests father us spiritually by saying the Mass and administering the sacraments, especially the Eucharist. They can do this only because their fatherhood is derived from God the Father. Just as we (and Protestants) don't hesitate to call our biological fathers "father," so we don't hesitate to honor our spiritual fathers with the same title of respect.

    The words of Jesus himself show that it was common practice among the Jews to refer to their spiritual forbears as "father."

(See Matt 3:9 and Luke 16:24.) Moreover, the early Christians continued this practice; they clearly did not take Christ's admonition in a literal sense either. St. Paul, for example, said that Abraham is "the father of us all" (Rom 4:16), meaning our father in the household of faith. St. Stephen, filled with the Holy Spirit, also called Abraham "father" (Acts 7:2). St. Paul refers to himself as the father of the Corinthian Christians, his converts, in 1 Cor 4:15, and calls Timothy "my true child in the faith" in 1 Tim 1:2, again revealing his spiritual fatherhood.

8. Read John Chapter 6, which takes place just before the Jewish feast of Passover. Why are so many Jews who are following Jesus scandalized by his words? (p.267) What was the immediate result of Jesus' discourse? Is John 6 asking us to be cannibals? Why not?

    The Jews were scandalized by Christ's outlandish request, namely eating His flesh and blood. The Mosaic Law forbade the drinking of blood. To consume the blood of an animal, not to mention a human, would have been a grave enough violation to be cast out from the people. It was considered an abomination.

    After Jesus had given His discourse, many of His followers left. This is important evidence that Jesus did not mean His words to be taken only figuratively. If so, He would have clarified His teaching so that none would leave over a simple misunderstanding. Instead, He allowed many to leave Him that day. His words were, and remain, hard words to take.

    Eating Jesus' Body and drinking His Blood is not cannibalism. Jesus says that it is the Spirit that gives life, not the flesh (John 6:63). We eat the Eucharist for spiritual sustenance, not physical sustenance. Again, the bread that becomes Jesus — the bread of life — is a fulfillment, on a spiritual level, of the Old Testament foreshadowing of the manna that was given to the Israelites as they wandered in the desert.

9. Can you think of a way to argue that Christ's command to eat his Body and drink his Blood should be taken symbolically? Then argue the opposite — that Christ meant what he said literally. Explain why the latter position is more tenable. (P.263-267)

Here is a Protestant argument against a literal interpretation of the Eucharist: "Christ often spoke using parables and symbolic language. He meant that we should try to become like Him, so much so that we will be one with Him. Obviously we all cannot eat the Body of Jesus nor drink His Blood. He would not have suggested cannibalism to his followers. Besides, Christ says, 'It is the spirit which gives life, the flesh is of no avail' (John 6:63). What He did at the Last Supper was meant to be taken symbolically."

Yes, Christ did speak in parables and use symbolic language, but consider some of those instances. He says, "I am the door," meaning one has to go through Him in order to have eternal life. He says, "I am the good shepherd," meaning He takes care of his flock. He guards us and searches for lost followers. He says, "I am the vine," meaning He is the source of life. We need to adhere to Him in order to stay alive eternally.

But what does "I am the bread of life" mean? It is not nearly so obvious. As Jesus gave his discourse on the "Bread of Life" He dealt with those who grumbled among themselves. As the discourse proceeded, Jesus did not clarify or explain how the bread was a symbol. Rather, with each objection, He emphasized more strongly how His flesh was "food indeed" and His blood "drink indeed" (John 6:55). Just before that He began his re-explanation with "truly, truly" or depending on the translation, "amen, amen" to indicate the seriousness of this proposition.

At the conclusion of the discourse many who had been followers left Him, never to follow again. Would they have rejected Him over this symbolic command? And if it were indeed symbolic, shouldn't Jesus have explained what He meant rather than have many leave due to a misunderstanding?

No, His words were not meant to be taken symbolically. It was a hard teaching but He said what He meant. What Christ did explain was that his flesh was not meant to provide physical sustenance, like the manna from heaven, but rather spiritual sustenance, as we continue on this pilgrimage that is our life on this earth.

10. What might you do if someone challenged you on a Catholic belief,

doctrine, or ritual and you did not have a good response?

*Admit that it is a good and interesting question, and that you don't
have an answer at the moment. Tell him that you would like to
answer the question but must first research the topic. You might also
say with confidence that the Catholic Church has been in existence for
two thousand years and that one can be sure that the question has
been studied and answered thoroughly. If it is someone that you will
not see in the future, tell them that the Catechism of the Catholic
Church is a good starting point for understanding the issue and that
there are many resources available that provide information from the
Catholic perspective. Remind him that he will not be able to trust a
non-Catholic resource to provide an adequate answer.*

*Above all be charitable. Display humility — admit that perhaps
you should know the answer but that learning is a lifelong process
and you have not had the opportunity to learn everything yet.*

11. What occurred at the first Passover? How did Jesus fulfill both
     roles, as the firstborn Son of God, and as the Lamb of God during
     His final Passover meal? (p.271-274)

*Read the Passover account in the book of Exodus, Chapters 11 and
12. At the first Passover, the angel of death was sent to kill the
firstborn sons of the Egyptians. The angel "passed over" the
homes of the Israelites, the ones who killed a lamb and sprinkled
the blood on the doorposts. Christ, the Lamb of God and the "firstborn" of God, instituted the Eucharist at His last Passover with His
apostles. The "firstborn" and the lamb were one in the same.
Christ is the fulfillment of the Passover sacrifice. By sharing His
Body and Blood in the Eucharist, we become brothers and sisters in
Christ.*

12. How does the ritual described in Leviticus foreshadow the Mass?
     (p.273)

*The people were to bring as an offering of wheat, wine, and an
unblemished lamb. The priest offered this to the Lord on behalf of
the people. At Mass, we also offer bread and wine. The priest con-
secrates them, and "by the consecration of the bread and wine*

there takes place a change of the whole substance of the bread into the substance of the body of Christ our Lord and of the whole substance of the wine into the substance of his blood" (see CCC 1376). This change is called transubstantiation. Christ Himself is the unblemished sacrificial lamb.

13. Read 1 Corinthians 11. How do Paul's instructions about the Eucharist support the Church's teaching? (p.274-275)

    Paul rebukes the community for eating the Lord's Supper in a way that is casual and disrespectful. He instructs them on how it ought to be done. In verse 29 he writes that "Anyone who eats and drinks without discerning the body eats and drinks judgment upon himself." The word "discern" means to perceive or determine, so anyone who does not recognize that the Body of Jesus is being offered in the Eucharist is in danger of Christ's judgment.

Chapter 13

1. Is Michael "sowing seeds of division amongst the brethren" as Pastor Brown asserts? (p.279) If not, how would you characterize his actions?

    No. Michael has simply answered challenges to his beliefs. Because there is a difference in opinion does not mean that anyone is being divisive. It is a mistake to agree to a belief, for the sake of unity, apart from the truth. Christians should seek truth and be charitable. There is no contradiction there.

2. Pastor Brown expresses concern for "his flock." (p.279) Does the flock belong to him, or is he a wolf in sheep's clothing? What do such men do?

    The flock is God's. We belong to God. For someone to suggest that they or someone else has a flock is flirting with the beliefs of a cult. Wolves in sheep's clothing are those people, either Catholic or non-Catholic, who lead believers astray. They scatter the flock.

3. If someone asked if you were "born again," how would you respond? (p.291) Read Michael's explanation. What does the Catechism say about baptism? Is it a symbol, or something more?

You ought to respond as Michael did, that you've been baptized. The "born again" emphasis among some Bible-only Christians is due to a misunderstanding of John 3. Read Acts Chapter 2, especially verse 38. Also read CCC 1262 — as Peter said on that feast of Pentecost in Jerusalem, baptism is for the forgiveness of sins and the one baptized will receive the Holy Spirit. Baptism is more than just a symbol; it truly washes away original sin and all personal sin.

4. What does the Bible have to say about infant baptism? (P.293-294)

The Bible says nothing explicitly about infant baptism. However, there are instances in the Bible of entire households being baptized (Acts 16:14-15 and Acts 16:29-33), and we have no reason to believe that children — or infants — were excluded. Earliest writings and records indicate that infant baptism was the norm.

In addition, Colossians 2:11-12 likens baptism to circumcision, which was performed on all adult converts to Judaism as well as all Jewish infants. Baptism is the spiritual re-birth that replaces circumcision, so likewise, it is administered to adult converts and all infants.

5. What is the difference between human tradition and Sacred Tradition? (P.294-295)

The important difference is that Sacred Tradition has been passed down from the Apostles. It is part of God's Word, and is therefore binding. Paul, in 1 Corinthians talked about what was passed on to him. Read 2 Thessalonians 2:15. Paul is referring here to binding (Sacred) Tradition. There are many examples of Sacred Tradition. The Mass, for example, is not explicitly described in the Bible, but it has been passed on to us from the time of the Apostles. The sacrament of Reconciliation, Holy Orders, the belief in Mary's perpetual virginity, her Assumption into heaven, the intercession of the saints — all these beliefs are implicit in Scripture, yet are only understood fully through the Sacred Tradition passed down to us from the Apostles.

Human tradition takes many forms. In the Mass, for example, many practices and customs have changed over the course of years — that women must wear their heads covered at Mass, that we kneel at a communion rail to receive the Eucharist, that girls are now permitted to assist the priest at Mass. We may not agree with certain changes in Church customs and practices, but we dare not insist that they are part of the Sacred Deposit of Faith, that which was passed on directly from Christ through the Apostles.

6. What is meant by intercession? (p.297-298) Is it unbiblical to pray to those in heaven for their intercession? Does Pastor Brown have a problem with intercessory prayer in and of itself? Explain the Catholic belief in the Communion of Saints.

    To intercede is to mediate or intervene on behalf of someone, to act as a go-between. It is not unbiblical to pray to the saints for their intercession. Pastor Brown, and fundamentalists in general, have no problem with the concept of intercession itself. They pray for one another, and it is usually woven into their worship service. What they do not do is ask for the intercession of the Saints in heaven.

    We Catholics believe in the "Communion of Saints." We know that as St. Paul says, nothing can separate us from the love of Christ, not even death. There are many texts in Scripture that can be cited to support this belief. Paul, writing to the Ephesians (2:19), teaches that the Christians are fellow citizens with the Saints. In Hebrews 12:1, he reminds us that the Saints in Heaven are watching over us, that "we are surrounded by so great a cloud of witnesses." Mark 12:26-27 shows Jesus explaining the resurrection to the Sadducees. He points out to them that God "is the God of the living, not the dead." After the death of our bodies, we will still remain members of the Body of Christ.

    There is one Church but three parts: The Church Militant is made up of those who are on earth, the Church Suffering is composed of those in Purgatory, and the Church Triumphant includes those who are now in heaven with God. We can pray for those in Purgatory. They can pray for us. We both can pray to members of the Church Triumphant — ask that they intercede with God on our behalf. Again, all Christians are part of the Body of Christ, with Christ as our Head. No part of the Body is "cut off" because of death.

Remember also how Michael O'Shea explains the role of the queen mother in the Old Testament Jewish kingdom. She interceded with the king on behalf of the people, just as Mary, the "Queen Mother of Heaven," does for us today with Jesus our King.

7. Do Catholics re-sacrifice Christ at each Mass? (p.299-300)

    No, the sacrifice of the Mass simply makes Christ's once-for-all sacrifice on Calvary present for us today. He is the everlasting sacrifice, a subtle yet crucial distinction. (See CCC 1366.)

8. What is the Immaculate Conception? (p.302) Pastor Brown claims that the Church invented this doctrine in 1854. (p.304) Is this true?

    The Immaculate Conception refers to Mary being born without the stain of original sin. (It does not refer to the Virgin Birth of Christ, which is a common misunderstanding.) The Immaculate Conception was not invented in 1854; however, that was the year the doctrine was formally defined. This is an important point. The Church often defines a belief formally only when a dispute or question arises. In the case of the Immaculate Conception, the Church was merely confirming what had been the Church's position through the centuries.

9. How do we Catholics explain our belief in the perpetual virginity of Mary? (p.303)

    The Blessed Mother conceived by the Holy Spirit — He is her true spouse. St. Joseph was her earthly husband and protector of the Holy Family. But, we know from the Annunciation that Mary had made a vow of virginity because she asked the angel how she was to conceive a child. If she had been planning to have marital relations with Joseph, the question would not make sense. (See Luke 1:34.) Also, Christ is referred to as "The son of Mary," not "A son of Mary." (Mark 6:3).

Protestants are averse to the idea that celibacy can be a virtue in serving Christ, so they try to disprove Mary's perpetual virginity by pointing out the references in the Bible to Jesus' "brothers." But, the word "brother" in the Bible is a term with a wide meaning, and is often used to describe a cousin or other relative.

10. Pastor Brown insists that if the Church is wrong about even one doctrine she teaches, then that calls into question everything the Church teaches. (p.303) Is this a valid argument? Why or why not?

This is a valid argument. If the Church were wrong in her teaching in one area it would call into question all that she teaches. We believe that the Holy Spirit guides the Church and leads her to all truth. She is protected from error when teaching on faith and morals.

It is true that individuals, even those with authority in the Church, have made mistakes. Church officials and those charged with teaching the Faith have certainly made mistakes or taught error at times. Some do so without realizing it and others are heretics who think they know better than the Church.

11. How does Michael (and how should you) answer any and all misinterpretations of Scripture?

Clearly and with charity. Help others to understand that the Catholic Church does have a thorough and reasonable interpretation of every passage in Scripture they question. Even if they don't agree with the Church's interpretation, you should be able to provide them with enough explanation and supporting passages to make them reconsider.

Epilogue

1. George apparently rejects all that Michael has explained to him about the Catholic Faith. (p.311) What lessons can we learn from this evident rejection, with respect to our efforts to evangelize others? Did Michael waste his time with George?

   Some will turn away from a presentation of the truth, at least initially, even when your words strike a chord of sense with them. It is very difficult to admit having been wrong, especially about deep-seated religious beliefs. The truth, however, cannot be forced on anyone. It has to be accepted with a change of heart, which takes time, and ultimately, God's grace. We often don't know the eventual results of our efforts to evangelize, but we can be sure of this — doing God's will and speaking His Truth in love is never a waste of time!

2. Do you know anyone like Uncle Matty? Would you consider him to be a "good" Catholic? (p.312-313)

   Just because someone is baptized into the Catholic Church doesn't mean he or she will always try to adhere to Church teachings. Some of the baptized truly do not know or understand Church teachings, sometimes due to poor catechesis. Others know and understand, but rebel against teachings with which they personally disagree. For adults, not being knowledgeable about Church teachings is often a weak excuse, with the ready availability of the Catechism and myriad other resources. It is our responsibility to inform our consciences.

3. Michael has no knowledge (at the end of the story) as to whether or not he has had any impact on the others. We see that Eli, at least, is greatly affected. (p.314-316) What lesson about evangelization is demonstrated here?

   You can speak the truth in love, and follow the promptings of the Holy Spirit, but still you will often not know the fruit that is borne from your actions. Just as when we sin, the Body of Christ is injured in ways we cannot even imagine, so when we proclaim

God's Truth we build up Christ's Body in ways we may never real-
ize on this earth.

4. Uncle Les's ultimate response to Michael's explanations is not
    divulged in the book. Do you think he has been challenged by
    Michael's beliefs? Now that Michael is out of the picture, will Uncle
    Les just put the whole episode behind him?

    At various points in the book, Uncle Les realizes he has no ade-
    quate response to Michael's presentations about the Catholic Faith.
    We also see that Les is a man of great faith, in dogged pursuit of
    the truth. We see his wife Pam expressing interest, and then his son
    Eli attending Mass on his own. It would be near impossible for Les
    to avoid considering the Catholic Faith over and over again, par-
    ticularly if his son converts. Although it would be difficult to
    reverse his deeply-held misconceptions about the Catholic Church,
    we can feel confident he will study and consider the issues involved
    thoroughly. This shows the "ripple effect" of our actions. While
    Les may have tried to forget about the information presented by
    Michael, he cannot ignore the conversion of his son.

To order additional copies of this
Discussion/Study Guide,
or to order copies of
A Philadelphia Catholic in King James's Court,
call toll-free:

1-800-932-3051